Free From M.E.

Permission

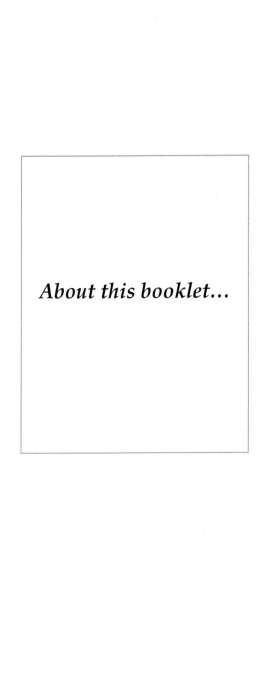

About this booklet...

I wrote this as a journal in 2005 after being ill with M.E. for nearly 3 years. I thought it would be of interest to close friends and family, so I printed 50 copies on my computer.

Over the last seven years so many people have heard my story and asked for a booklet that I have given out over 500 copies. It has even been translated into Spanish for some friends to take to Cuba.

I've had such a lot of feedback from people who have read and been encouraged by this story, that I decided to publish it in the hope that it will reach even more people.

Debbie Plura 2012

About M.E. ...

The following is taken from the Sheffield M.E.
Group website

‶ M.E. is an illness which affects the brain, muscles
and nervous system.

There is no cure or simple treatment

One study showed that 20% of people go on to make
a complete recovery within 2 years.

Most people with M.E. show some degree of
improvement over a period of time, though often
over years rather than months. But health and
functioning rarely return to the individual's previous
level of health, and most of those who feel relatively
recovered stabilise at a lower level of functioning
than before the start of their illness. ″

http://www.sheffieldmegroup.co.uk

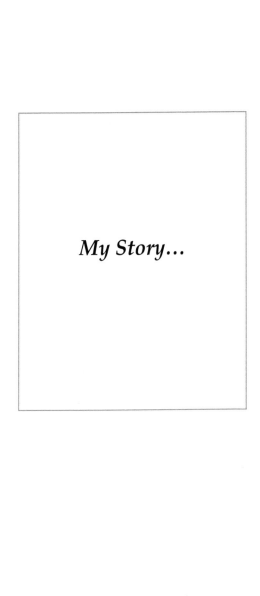

My Story...

Hi,

My name is Debbie. I am 43 years old. I live in Sheffield with my husband Martin and 3 sons James 18, Joe 14 and Tom who is 12. I work as a Pharmacy assistant 2 days a week and, up to the summer of 2002, I had a fairly active home and social life.

The problem started with a tummy bug in July almost three years ago. This left me feeling very dizzy, sick and exhausted. People usually recover from viruses over a short period of time but I found that as the weeks and months went on I didn't feel better at all; in fact I was getting worse.

A year later, after a few trips to the doctor and a series of blood tests, I was diagnosed with Myalgic Encephalomyelitis (M.E.); also known as Chronic Fatigue Syndrome (C.F.S.).

My symptoms varied from day to day with mornings being the worst time. The following are just some of the ways that M.E. affected my every day life:

Work – I worked in the Pharmacy all day Thursdays and Fridays. I usually had to go to bed around 9pm those nights but woke up feeling drained the next morning, as if I hadn't slept at all. Mornings at work usually consisted of blurred vision and fatigued muscles (the walk from the counter, up one step and into the dispensary was really hard work). I felt dizzy, not quite there and often forgot what I was doing, or how to do a simple task. I had to focus very hard on one thing at a time. My self-confidence tended to be very low on a bad day at work; I felt like I couldn't get anything right.

Church – it was very hard to focus on worshipping God or listening to sermons, especially when I was particularly dizzy or in pain. Even chatting to people after the service was so tiring.

Home – Housework was difficult. Wiping the table down with a damp cloth would make my muscles feel like I'd been doing press-ups all day. A friend used to come and clean the house as it was too exhausting for me, and for the last few months I have paid James to do it, as he needed to earn some money. I used to feel guilty when, after a day at work, Martin had to do the jobs that I would usually do, and then he would look so tired. I also felt bad when I couldn't do the things with the boys that I wanted to do.

It was frustrating when I used to get my words mixed up trying to explain something to someone. I was very sensitive to noise. Scrolling and reading things on the computer made me dizzy. A sleep in the afternoon was essential to be able to complete the rest of the day. I always had a sore throat, swollen glands and was susceptible to infections. I was very forgetful too.

I didn't do big family-sized shopping trips any more as it made me feel dizzy, sick and as if my legs weren't working properly. It made me feel exhausted for the rest of the day.

Exercise – anything more than a stroll left me feeling achy and wobbly-limbed for a couple of days, or sometimes weeks afterwards.

I had many different tests at the hospital to rule out all sorts of illnesses and nothing was found to be the cause of the symptoms. I wasn't offered any real help or treatment. My GP was quite nice and understanding but all he could offer me was antidepressants, which I never accepted because I knew I wasn't depressed. I was ill and fed-up with feeling so ill and tired, but I wasn't depressed.

The Conference

In March 2005 a friend called Janet, asked me to go with her to a healing conference. The speakers, Noel and Denise Dunn from Canada, were teaching on how to pray for the sick. I'd always had an interest in healing, and I prayed that God would show me whether I should go to the conference or not.

Eventually I decided that there would be no way that I could concentrate on four days of teaching, and then of course I would need to put it into practice. It felt like it would be just too much to cope with and I knew that it would take weeks to get over that level of concentration. Our son James said he would go with Janet, as he wanted to learn about healing too.

Friday, the first day of the conference

I had to come home from work at lunchtime today, as I'd got a tummy bug and couldn't carry on. It was a good job I hadn't intended going to the conference! I got home about 1.15pm and slept on the settee until bedtime, hardly able to rouse myself to get up, even for drinks. I vaguely remember James coming home and saying how great the teaching at the conference was.

Day 2 of the conference

Today I woke at 9am still feeling ghastly, and just had a drink for breakfast. By lunchtime I was just about ready to have another sleep when the phone rang. It was James ringing from the conference.

He said "Mum, the lady that was speaking this morning said 'if you want healing you've got to be where the anointing is', so you'd better get over here straight away."

So, I had a decision to make. On the one hand I felt too ill to go and be healed. On the other hand, what if God was guiding James to tell me to go, and I didn't? So I went!

Martin drove me there as I was not feeling well enough to drive. I'd had no lunch and decided it would be a good idea to have a banana to help me to concentrate. I ate half of it and couldn't stomach any more. It seemed a stupid idea to go out when I felt that rough!

There were only 30-40 people at the conference but the teaching was excellent. The thing that spoke to me most that day, was that sin and sickness were both treated the same by Jesus - He removed them. It was not any harder for Jesus to heal the sick than to forgive people their sins. We have made it that way with our wrong thinking.

Praise the Lord, O my soul, and forget not all his benefits – who forgives all your sins and heals all your diseases,
Psalm 103, verses 2-3

In the New Testament Jesus often spoke about the forgiveness of sin and healing of sickness in the same stories. One is not harder or easier than the other for Him to do. Just as we often think that a common cold would be easier for Him to heal than terminal cancer. That is not true either.

Some other good points that day reminded us that all sickness is from the devil and that God wants us to be well now and not 'in His timing', as I used to think. God is a good God who wants His children well and whole all the time. The devil is evil and wants us to live in sickness and bondage all the time. So God's timing is always NOW and His will is always for us to be well!

I was really able to hear and take in all that was being said that afternoon and was excited about going back the next day to hear more. When I got home Martin had cooked a meal which I ate with no problem and really enjoyed. I hadn't even been prayed for but God had healed the tummy bug anyway!

Day 3 of the conference

The next day was Sunday, we had church in the morning and a leaders' meeting in the evening. During the service I was able to concentrate on the worship time and communion, which was so much more meaningful to me because we'd been learning the previous day just what Jesus had achieved when He died on that cross. Then I went downstairs to teach some of the teenagers. This was a first time for us as a group and I remember asking them to pray that God would heal me during the afternoon meeting.

The afternoon teaching was as good as the day before. I realised that I had been too accepting of my illness and not living in the belief of God's word, which says things like: *by his wounds you have been healed* (1 Peter 2 verse 24), and Jesus himself said: *I have come that they may have life, and have it to the full.* (John 10 verse 10).
No way was my life of illness a life to the full!

The lady who was teaching said, "If any of you have ever had a scripture given to you about your healing, you need to believe it because it has got to come to pass. The bible says that God's word never returns to Him empty (Isaiah 55 verse 11). So if God has promised you something, believe it, because He is a faithful God who never goes back on His word."

As I heard that, I remembered that I'd been given a scripture from our pastor Paul a year or so previously. I fished the piece of paper out of my bible and read it:

I will restore you to health and heal your wounds
Jeremiah chapter 30, verse 17

As I read this I realised that Janet, who had invited me to the conference, had also given me this scripture a few months ago. So I decided to do as the lady said and believe that this was God speaking to me through His word, and what He has said must come into being.

At the same time I got very angry at the devil for putting me and my family through this for the last 3 years. In my head I was stamping my feet and telling Satan that enough is enough, his time has ended; I wasn't putting up with it any more.

After the talk people were invited to go forward for prayer. When it was my turn to be prayed for, rather than saying "Please pray for me to be healed from M.E." which is what I had planned to say, I found myself saying "I believe I've been healed from M.E. this afternoon, will you pray for me?"

Now I can't say that I felt anything when I was being prayed for. I can't even remember what was prayed. I do remember not being able to stand any longer and falling to the floor, shaking with the power of God and experiencing a feeling of deep peace.

When I got up and went to sit down I didn't feel like talking to people, I knew God had done something and it was too precious to use mere words at that time.

Usually by mid-afternoon, I would be desperate for a sleep, but that afternoon I felt alive and buzzing. We went straight from the conference to a leaders' meeting at Janet's house. The leaders' meeting finished too late for us to go to the evening conference, but I felt that I probably didn't need to be there anyway.

Day 4 of the conference

I woke up full of excitement on Monday, wondering
what was going to happen today. I decided to take
the dog for a walk. Previously I had only been able to
take her out for 5-10 minutes before I would start to
feel dizzy and exhausted. In fact I hadn't walked
Amber for well over a year, as one day I got about
200 meters' down the road with her and just stood
there, almost like I'd forgotten how to walk. My
brain wasn't sending the right messages to my legs.
It only lasted a few seconds but it frightened me and
I didn't take her out on my own again.

Today I took her for 30 minutes, with a 5-minute sit
down on the park bench before coming back. When I
got back my legs felt quite wobbly, but it wasn't the
usual muscle aches I'd had before; this was because
the muscles were being used. It felt so good! I felt like
I'd got more energy, quite an alien feeling to me!

Today's meetings were afternoon and evening, so
after an early lunch, I decided that I'd better have a
sleep before I went to the afternoon meeting or I'd
never last the day. I lay down on the settee and could
not get off to sleep, so I gave up. I eventually realised
that I didn't need a sleep because I was healed.
Sleeping in the afternoon was just something I'd got
used to doing.

This was the last day of the conference and I went to both afternoon and evening sessions, which were again very helpful. I was able to take in all that was said and cook a meal for the family between sessions. I still hadn't discussed much of this with anyone, except a bit with James. It was too big and I didn't want anyone to put the dampers on anything that had been done. Besides, I figured that people would soon start to see a difference in me, so although I did say in yesterday's leaders' meeting I'd been prayed for, I didn't tell anyone how different I felt.

The next few days...

Tuesday

I woke up feeling quite refreshed. I wasn't used to that; I usually woke up feeling just as exhausted as I did when I went to bed. I suppose anyone would have been tired after such a hectic weekend and the little bit of tiredness I felt today was just ordinary tiredness, not exhaustion.

I took Amber for a 20 minute walk and prayed for her knee which was operated on last summer but still had a lot of stiffness in it. We noticed a real difference in the knee over the next few days.

I had the runs this morning but felt very clearly God saying to me that it's nothing to worry about; it's just my body getting rid of the rubbish, like a cleansing. When I went in the kitchen to make my usual morning coffee, God told me not to, so I had water instead. This happened again later and when I was making lunch of vegetable soup and toast, He said "not the bread, just vegetables and water". So I prayed about this and felt I should just have fruit, vegetables and water but didn't know how long for.

I asked God to confirm this in some way by teatime. When we sat down to eat, my son Joe noticed just the veg on my plate and asked me about it. I told him what had been going on. Just as I was about to put the first forkful in my mouth, Joe said "Daniel".

Of course he was thinking of Daniel in the bible who only ate vegetables. After 10 days of eating like this he was found to look, and to be, fitter than the people who ate the rich food from the king's table. So there was the confirmation and the amount of days I was to do it for. God's timing is always perfect!

Wednesday
I went to Tesco on my own and did a large family-sized shop with no dizziness or fatigue.
Because I'd been drinking 4-6 mugs of coffee a day until yesterday, I had expected to get a caffeine withdrawal headache, but I didn't have any withdrawal symptoms whatsoever!

Thursday and Friday
These were my first days at work since I'd been healed and I still hadn't really told anyone but my family what had happened. Within minutes of arriving at work both Chris and Jayne said how well I was looking, so I told them the good news. I worked with a clear head and felt good all day.

Saturday

Today I had a lovely surprise. Around 11am I started to feel very hot, I was burning up inside. My temperature was perfectly normal when I tested it. The burning lasted for around an hour and then it went, but afterwards I was filled with more energy than I can remember ever having. I went outside and did an hour's gardening, swept the whole patio, washed and dried a load of pots, did my accounts on the computer and did 3 loads of washing. Then I changed all the cushion covers in the dining room and made enough ratatouille for 8 servings and was still looking around for things to do. I felt great and actually enjoyed doing the work, because I could! By 9pm I felt really tired, but happy because it was normal tiredness and not the exhaustion that made me feel like I couldn't go on any longer.

Sunday

I got up feeling great – happy, full of joy and looking forward to going to church. I started to laugh when I imagined ringing my friend Jean in Southampton and saying "Are you sitting down?" before telling her what had happened.

I shared what had happened with the church this morning and everyone was very happy for me and said how well I looked. We went to the Xstatic youth meeting this evening. It was noisy, as usual, but even the loud noise didn't hurt my ears as it had before.

Monday

Usually I dread having visitors of any sort because everything is just too much like hard work and the next few days are spent recovering from it. This doesn't mean I don't want to see people (before you all fall out with me) it just means that it's draining and exhausting. Today, both of my sisters and my 2-year-old great nephew were coming for the day. Before they came I decided the grout in the bathroom tiles needed cleaning. That took me an hour and would usually be enough to ground me for the rest of the day, but not now. I continued pottering and chatted to Jean on the phone (she was sitting down when I told her the news).

We had a nice day and went to Heeley City Farm to see the animals after lunch. My family left around 3pm and I made a few phone calls – something that I rarely did before – and made tea.

After tea, we went shopping before picking Joe up from work. I still had energy left and wasn't drained or needing to recover from my busy day. Wow!

Tuesday

I woke today feeling refreshed. I could get up within a few minutes of waking and even hold a conversation during breakfast, both of which I could not do before. I did a load of typing for this testimony, and then went shopping to treat my new slimmer self to some clothes, having lost 4lb this week.

By the end of the second week
I felt great, fighting fit, full of energy and enthusiasm. Work this week was fine and many people commented on how well I looked.

Martin has noticed a big difference in my thought processes; they're much faster. I'm getting on and doing jobs and enjoying the sense that I can do them without paying the price for it.

People say things like "You've got your sparkle back", or "The life's back in your eyes." One person said, "Before, you looked like a careworn old lady, now you look like a carefree little girl."

My concentration and memory are greatly improved. I drove to Thoresby Craft Fair and back, about 50 miles in all, without any problems or tiredness. I've felt tired out by about bed time but the tiredness was normal tiredness not the 'M.E. exhaustion'. My muscles tell me they haven't been used when I do stuff, but I don't have the M.E. muscle aches that can last for weeks and not be relieved by tablets.

My creativeness has returned. I used to really struggle to try to think of things like what to get people for birthdays, or what we will eat each day, but that is no longer a problem.

Spiritually, I want to keep learning more and more of God's word and applying it to my life. I feel closer to God than I've felt for a long time. It's great to praise and worship Him now because I can close my eyes without holding on to the chair in front of me. (Before, I was so dizzy that I felt I would fall over if I closed my eyes). I can also raise my arms during worship without getting pins and needles and the muscle aches that I used to get after about 15 seconds.

Other symptoms that have disappeared are the permanent sore throats, swollen glands, heavy, weak limbs and low moods. My temperature is normal and I don't have the intermittent flu-like feelings anymore. Also the clumsiness, dropping things, sleepiness and weird thoughts have completely gone.

Three weeks after I'd been healed

I went to meet Jean at the railway station café before she returned to Southampton. She hadn't seen me for some months and looked past me as I walked through the door to meet her. She had been expecting to see the "careworn old lady" that I had been and was so surprised when I got to her table. She said "You've got such a spring in your step, I didn't recognise you!"

She, like everyone else, was amazed at the difference in me. But then, we have an amazing God don't we?

I hope that as you've read this journal it has shown you that God still heals today, and He wants to heal you too. Father God sent His son Jesus to die on the cross for you, so that you can be forgiven from all your sins and healed of all your sicknesses.

Debbie   May 2005

But that's not the end of the story...

The last 7 years –
life to the full…

At the same time that the M.E. was healed, I was also healed of a viral disease I'd had for about 25 years.

Two or three times a year I would start to feel tired and have shooting pains in the nerves of my hands, arms or ears. After a few days an area of blister-like spots would erupt in that area, they would disappear over the next five or six days. I was told that this was caused by the same herpes type virus which causes cold sores. I never had another outbreak since the M.E. was healed. The frequent sicknesses and viruses went, and in the last seven years I have only had two colds.

Sometimes when I am feeling run down or fighting something off, the M.E. type symptoms come back but I know that's just the enemy trying to see if I will accept the illness back, and of course I don't. I know I was healed by the work of the Cross, I know that Jesus took my sickness upon Himself, so why would I take it back?

The last seven years have been so exciting because I've seen some of the plans and purposes that God has for my life come into reality!

In 2007 Janet and I set up the first Healing Rooms in Sheffield. We meet in the upper room of the Big Tree Pub in Woodseats. We have seen many people healed, delivered, set free and saved. Among many other healings, I have been very privileged to pray for others who have had M.E. and see them completely healed, thank you Jesus!

I recently started preaching about healing in my own church and have seen people healed of breast lump, shoulder problems, painful backs, a hand injury and a kidney infection. I've seen eyesight restored and emotional problems dealt with because people have responded to the teaching about Jesus being their healer.

The sermons were recorded and I sent them to my friend Jean in Southampton. She then lent them to someone from her church who had suffered from endometriosis for 15 years. This lady listened to God's word and then asked her church to pray for her. Her healing was confirmed at the next hospital check-up. I have never met her but she told Jean that listening to those sermons changed her life. The same lady was also healed of Fibromyalgia a few months after her first healing.

I am so excited when I hear stories like that because it proves that it was God, and that He is backing up His word with signs and wonders, as He says He will do.

*Then the disciples went out and preached
everywhere, and the Lord worked with them and
confirmed his word by the signs that accompanied it.
Mark chapter 16 verse 20*

I have recently set up a ministry called Touch Heal
Free because that is what God has called me to do.
This is His plan and purpose for my life. What I
myself received from God is what He now wants me
to do for others, as He told His disciples:

*Heal the sick, raise the dead,
cleanse those who have leprosy, drive out demons.
Freely you have received, freely give.
Matthew chapter 10 verse 8*

In the UK I have shared my testimony at many
different venues and have prayed for the sick
afterwards and seen them healed. I'll be continuing
to hold healing meetings for the sick, especially M.E.
sufferers.

Over the last few years I have been to Zimbabwe,
Uganda and Denmark. People are often healed as
they hear the teaching about healing.

I have seen all kinds of sicknesses healed, such as a baby with malaria, a woman with pneumonia, and a man who could not speak after suffering a stroke months before. He woke up the next morning and was able to speak some words, I'm told he just keeps improving and the other symptoms of the stroke were healed too. A woman with a broken leg was completely healed and danced with stiletto shoes on in church the next day.

It's wonderful to be part of God's plan and see so many lives change around the world. This year I have plans to go to back to Zimbabwe and Uganda, as well as visit Kenya and India.

Also this year, my challenges are to complete a book about my experiences and produce a series of CD's about healing. These will be available through my website. All money raised from books, teaching CD's and offerings at meetings will go towards trips to Third World countries, to bring the message of hope and healing to the poor.

God's love and grace towards me is amazing. I know that now I am living my life to the full, which is what He intended.

I hope this story has blessed and encouraged you. What God has done in me is what He wants for everybody. He doesn't want to see His children sick. He came that we can have life in all its fullness!

Do get in touch if you would like to know more about anything you've read in this booklet.

If you would like me to come and talk to your group, preach or pray for people you know who are sick, I'd love to hear from you.

Love

Debbie

Email debbieplura@hotmail.com
Website www.touchhealfree.net

Woodseats Healing Rooms
Visit www.woodseatshealingrooms.org
You can leave a confidential message on their answer phone: 0114 3600616

Printed in Great Britain
by Amazon.co.uk, Ltd.,
Marston Gate.